Journey of Flavours
for Senses

Vasim Shaikh

BookLeaf Publishing
India | USA | UK

Presentation by *BookLeaf Publishing*

Web: www.bookleafpub.com

E-mail: info@bookleafpub.com

ISBN: 9789363313866

First edition 2024

To all those who visualize the world through their minds and paint their destiny with the vivid strokes of their imagination,

Your vision is the canvas on which the future is crafted. Your dreams are the colors that bring life to the otherwise monochrome reality. In the quiet moments of reflection and the bold acts of creation, you redefine what is possible and inspire us all to see beyond the horizon.

With deepest admiration and respect,

Vasim Shaikh

ACKNOWLEDGEMENT

Thank you, world, for allowing me to observe and interpret your beauty. Through the flow of words, I've been able to build a bridge between the real and the ideal. Each poem is a testament to this journey, inspired by the images captured by Vasim Shaikh, a.k.a. Beardboss.

With gratitude,
Vasim Shaikh

PREFACE

Poetry in Motion is a journey into the heart of the visual world, captured and interpreted by Vasim Shaikh, known to many as Beardboss. Each poem in this collection is a testament to the beauty and power of imagery, reflecting the intricate dance between sight and word. As an accomplished photographer, Vasim's lens has always been his primary tool for storytelling, but through this book, he reveals another layer of his artistic soul: his poetic voice.

Inspired by the images he has captured, these poems are more than just descriptions—they are reflections, emotions, and narratives that transcend the visual to touch the very essence of what it means to observe and to feel. Each photograph is a spark, igniting a cascade of words that flow seamlessly into verses, creating a unique tapestry of visual and poetic art.

In "Poetry in Motion", you will find a diverse array of themes and subjects, each poem mirroring the depth and breadth of Vasim's photographic portfolio. From serene landscapes to candid portraits, from the bustling energy of urban life to the quiet solitude of nature, each image is reimagined through the lens of poetry.

This collection is not just a book of poems; it is an invitation to see the world through Vasim's eyes and to experience the profound connections between what we see and what we feel.

As you turn each page, allow yourself to be transported into the moments captured by Vasim's camera, and let his words guide you through the emotions and stories that lie within. Poetry in Motion is a celebration of the symbiosis between visual and literary art, and it is my hope that it inspires you to see the world with a renewed sense of wonder and appreciation.

Welcome to the world of Vasim Shaikh, where every image is a poem, and every poem is an image in motion.

— Vasim Shaikh, a.k.a. Beardboss

CONTENTS

Inner Child

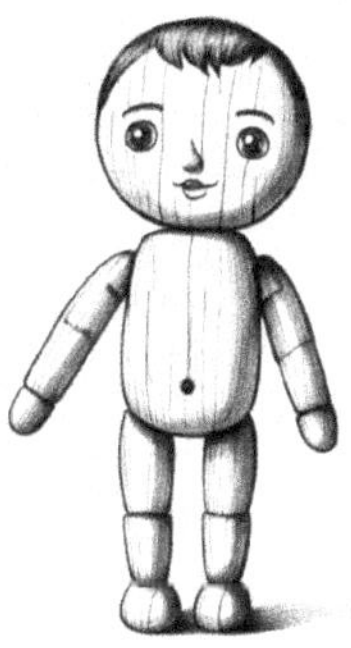

In the quiet corners of my mind,
Lives a child, untouched by time.
Eyes wide with wonder, heart pure and free,
Dancing in the dreams of who I used to be.

Whispers of laughter, echoes of play,
Guide my grown-up footsteps each day.
In every smile and tear I've shed,
My inner child lives on, well-fed.

Through trials and triumphs, joy and strife,
That little spark breathes life into my life.
Forever young, with spirit bright,
My inner child, my guiding light.

#beardboss

Cactus on the rocks

Roots embrace the ancient stone,
In solitude, it's not alone.
Life finds a path, defies the odds,
A quiet hymn to nature's gods.

Silent sentinels rise,
Green arms reach toward the skies,
On the stone wall's face,
Cactus finds its steady place.

Spiny fingers, bold and bright,
In the scorching desert light,
Against the rock, it stands alone,
Nature's strength in every stone.

#beardboss

Carpet of the heavens

On ancient stones, the green moss grows,
In silent shades where time flows slow.
Whispers of years in soft embrace,
Nature's touch on a rugged face.

Life in stillness, quietly spreads,
A living quilt where secrets are fed.
Emerald hues on weathered grey,
Beauty thrives in a tranquil display.

#beardboss

Balance of the Stones

In stillness, stones find harmony,
Each balance a quiet decree.
Life, like rocks in careful pose,
Stands firm through highs and lows.

With patience, each stone aligns,
Echoing life's silent signs.
Steady hands and hearts entwine,
Crafting balance, pure and fine.

Each stone a story, weathered and true,
Teaching lessons in the view.
In balance, we find our way,
Stone by stone, day by day.

#beardboss

The Flying Dragon

A brass dragonfly, immortal in flight,
Wings of metal, gleaming in the light.
Frozen in time, yet whispering tales,
Of summer breezes and tranquil trails.

Perched on petals, eternal and still,
Embodying nature's delicate thrill.
In the garden of memory, it forever stays,
A symbol of life's ephemeral days.

Crafted with care, enduring the years,
A silent witness to joys and tears.
The brass dragonfly, timeless and bright,
A beacon of grace in the twilight.

#beardboss

Swing or Stay

Beneath the blooming creeper's tender spread,
A swing and bench, both soaking in the rain,
In whispers soft, their silent words were said,
Each envying the other's sweet domain.

The swing did sway with gentle, rhythmic grace,
Dreaming of the bench's steadfast calm,
While the bench admired the swing's free space,
Longing for the swing's serene, wet balm.

The creeper, lush with blossoms, hung above,
Eavesdropping on their soft, envious sighs,
Each drop of rain, a tear, a tale of love,
Binding their dreams beneath the weeping skies.

In this serene, wet world, a quiet dance,
The swing and bench, in rain-soaked elegance.

#beardboss

Dawn of a City

As dawn awakens the city's heart,
A golden ray plays its part.
On a quiet street, the world is still,
Sunbeams dance on windowsills.

Life stirs gently in the morning light,
Shadows retreat, giving up the night.
Reflections whisper tales untold,
Of dreams and hopes in hues of gold.

Each beam a promise, bright and true,
In every pane, a chance anew.
The city breathes, alive with grace,
Embracing the sun's warm embrace.

#beardboss

Silent Mystic

In the heart of the forest, where shadows dance,
Lives a woman with a mystical trance.
Her vibrant spirit, wild and free,
Holds secrets of the ancient tree.

She whispers to the birds in flight,
Guides the wolves through the night.
With a touch as soft as morning dew,
She heals the old, the weak, the new.

Her voice, a melody, gentle and kind,
Speaks to the animals, heart and mind.
She mends their wounds, soothes their fears,
With a soul that listens, a heart that hears.

In her eyes, the universe unfolds,
A story of love, timeless and bold.
For she is the guardian, the healer divine,
Connecting all creatures, heart, soul, and mind.

#beardboss

Balloon of Dreams

Floating thoughts on silk threads glide,
In a hot air balloon, through vast skies wide.
To a realm where dreams dare to dance,
And extraordinary imaginations take their
chance.

Clouds like whispers softly speak,
Of lands where wonders boldly peek.
Mountains of marvel, rivers of rhyme,
In this world beyond the edge of time.

Colors blend in surreal hues,
As fantasies paint a vivid muse.
Onward we soar, hearts unchained,
In this sky where magic is unrestrained.

Each fleeting thought a spark, a flame,
In a universe where the wildest dreams
proclaim.
Here in this balloon, high and free,
We drift in extraordinary ecstasy.

#beardboss

Silence in the City

In the city that never rests, where dreams take flight,
A group of minds, brilliant, weaving through the night.
Every silence a symphony, thoughts loud and deep,
In the heart of Bombay, where inspirations leap.

Eyes gleam with stories, yet words stay withheld,
In quiet moments, creativity is compelled.
From the bustling streets to the quiet bays,
Their silence speaks in mysterious ways.

Each pause, a masterpiece, each breath a stroke,
In the city's rhythm, where visions provoke.
Silent musings, a canvas in the air,
Bombay's creative souls, a bond beyond
compare.

#beardboss

Steamy Affair

In the quiet morn, a generator hums,
Its twin exhausts a gentle whisper,
Rain falls softly, each droplet drums,
Against the metal, a dance crisper.

Steam rises, a fleeting affair,
Raindrops meet the warmth in grace,
Tiny clouds ascend the air,
A brief romance in a hidden place.

Mingling moments, mist and heat,
In the heart of the early day,
A transient love, pure and sweet,
In the steam, they find their way.

#beardboss

Eternal Flowers

Beneath the strokes of vivid orange hue,
In a vase, the flowers silently grew.
Creepers twine, a tender embrace,
Adding grace to their porcelain space.

Silent witness in a room aglow,
To whispered words and emotions' flow.
A canvas of life, in watercolor framed,
Bearing witness to joys unnamed.

Each petal a listener, each leaf a friend,
In the quiet of the room, emotions blend.
Through laughter and tears, the flowers stand,
An eternal witness, brush in hand.

#beardboss

Riding towards the light

Emerging from shadows, through the tunnel we ride,
Darkness recedes, where new hopes abide.
With each pedal forward, we break the night,
Eyes fixed on the horizon, seeking the light.

Rebooting our spirits, weary hearts renew,
Breathing in freedom, skies painted blue.
Rejuvenated souls, like dawn's first gleam,
Riding towards the light, embracing the dream.

#beardboss

Eternal Rose

In gardens where the whispers play,
A red rose blooms in the light of day.
Its petals soft, a velvet touch,
A symbol speaking love so much.

Timeless beauty, pure and bright,
Eternal love in crimson light.
With every thorn, a pledge so true,
Forever's promise bound in hue.

A gentle breeze, a silent sigh,
Red rose in bloom, beneath the sky.
A tale of hearts, forever spun,
Eternal love, forever one.

#beardboss

Aqua Bubble

In an aqua world, so clear and bright,
Colorful fishes dance in the light.
Through crystal waters, they glide and sway,
With fins like rainbows, they play all day.

A waterfall's chain of bubbles descends,
Creating ripples where the joy never ends.
They chase and dart, in a gleeful race,
Bubbles bursting into a splashing embrace.

Gold and silver, in hues so bold,
Stories of the deep, these waters hold.
In this serene, enchanted domain,
Fishes and bubbles in harmony remain.

#beardboss

Mirrors and door

Mirror, mirror on the wall,
Open the door beyond the call,
Show me worlds unseen, untold,
Where dreams and secrets dare unfold.

Through your glass, a portal clear,
Lies the magic, distant, near,
Realms of wonder, vast and grand,
Await beyond your silvery strand.

Glimpse of skies in colors bright,
Stars that twinkle through the night,
Whispers of a distant land,
Revealed by your reflective hand.

Mirror, mirror, guide my way,
To the realms where fantasies play,
Beyond the surface, deep and wide,
Unlock the wonders that inside reside.

#beardboss

Life in a Bottle

In a corner where the city's heart beats fast,
A bottle of water stands, memories cast.
Silent and still, yet brimming with might,
It nurtures white flowers, pure and bright.

Amid the chaos, in concrete's embrace,
Life unfurls gently, in this sacred place.
White petals whisper, in the hush of the night,
Of the bottle's gift, a humble, quiet light.

Each drop a promise, each sip a dream,
In the rush of life, a soft, gentle stream.
Blooming in a corner, unnoticed, unseen,
White flowers thrive, in a world so serene.

For in the bustle, where moments often stray,
A bottle of water breathes life, every day.
And though the city never seems to rest,
In that corner, nature finds its nest.

#beardboss

Flints in a Bottle

In Fort Bastian's shadowed halls, a legend old,
A pharaoh's essence in a bottle of gold,
Fragrance whispers tales of ancient lore,
Mystical powers locked behind a door.

Scents of myrrh and incense fill the air,
Echoes of Egypt, a kingdom so rare,
Within the glass, his spirit confined,
A relic of time, both sacred and blind.

Mystic winds swirl, secrets they keep,
Guarding the pharaoh in an eternal sleep,
Fort Bastian stands, a sentinel so bold,
Protecting the bottle and the pharaoh's soul.

#beardboss

Skyvilla

In the city's heart, a skyscraper soars high,
Piercing the heavens, touching the sky.
Steel and glass in majestic grace,
A modern marvel, a heavenly place.

Amongst the clouds, its peak resides,
Where dreams ascend and hope abides.
A lofty home, where souls can rest,
In a celestial haven, truly blessed.

Above the bustle, serene and free,
A sanctuary in the urban sea.
A beacon of light, a tranquil retreat,
In the city's embrace, heaven's seat.

#beardboss

Feathers and Flickers

In shadows deep, a lamp adorned,
With feathers soft, by mystics sworn.
Its flickering light, a dance so bright,
Unveils the tales of gods at night.

Whispers weave through silent air,
Echoes of legends, bold and rare.
From distant lands, where deities dwell,
The lamp's soft glow begins to tell.

Each feathered plume, a story holds,
Of ancient times, in lands of gold.
A divine realm where fates entwine,
Unfolding secrets, old and fine.

Its light, a bridge to worlds unseen,
Where mortals meet the gods serene.
In every flicker, dreams take flight,
Mysteries bloom in the soft moonlight.

Oh, lamp of wonder, guide us through,
With tales of gods, both old and new.
In your gentle, gleaming trance,
Let us in your stories dance.

#beardboss

Stairway to Gods

Staircase by the Bastian Stone Wall"

Carved in ancient stone, the staircase winds,
By Bastian's wall where history binds.
Each step echoes tales of days gone by,
Leading to realms where the Greek gods lie.

Marble whispers underfoot so old,
Stories of gods in hues of gold.
Zeus's thunder and Athena's grace,
Await at the summit, in a timeless place.

I climb through shadows, myths unfold,
The air grows thick with secrets told.
At the peak, the heavens greet my eyes,
A world of gods beneath the skies.

#beardboss

Carpe-diem

On a carpet woven long and grand,
In a corridor, through time it spans,
A royal welcome, a gentle glide,
Step forth, let dreams take flight inside.

Each thread a tale, a whispered lore,
Of kings and queens who walked before,
Velvet touch beneath your feet,
Invites you to a world so sweet.

Gaze ahead, the path unfurls,
A journey into mystic worlds,
Fantasy in every stride,
On this carpet, dreams collide.

Majestic hues, in patterns old,
Stories in the fabric told,
Walk the length, embrace the sight,
And take a flight of pure delight.

#beardboss

Patience and Grace

In a quiet corner, the bonsai stands,
Graceful and still, shaped by careful hands.
Each leaf whispers tales of time so slow,
Of seasons passed, and winds that blow.

In patience, it grows, inch by inch,
Teaching us that time doesn't flinch.
With roots deep and branches wide,
It waits, content, as the years glide.

A symbol of grace, a lesson in time,
The bonsai whispers in a voice so fine—
"Rushed are the days, but slow is the art,
To truly grow, you must take part."

#beardboss

The Chef Mode

In the depths of the wardrobe, it lay,
An old chef coat, forgotten, tucked away,
Dusty threads, once crisp and bright,
Now yearned for the kitchen's glowing light.

With a rustle, it stirred from its slumber deep,
Excitement brewing, no more to sleep,
Memories of dishes crafted with care,
Now ready to dance in the kitchen's warm air.

Buttons fastened, sleeves rolled tight,
It gleamed with pride, pure white,
Back in action, full force and flame,
An old chef coat, reclaiming its name.

#beardboss

Knives' Tale

In the drawer where the chefs' tools sleep,
The knives awake from their silent keep.
Paring Knife boasts, "I'm sharp and sly,
I slice through apples without a cry."

Santoku grins, "I'm sleek and fine,
I cut through veggies like they're wine."
Cleaver chuckles, "You're all so sweet,
But bones and meat are my favorite treat."

Chef's Knife gleams, "I'm the star of the show,
From mincing to dicing, I steal the flow."
Bread Knife yawns, "I don't need the fame,
But slicing through crust is my claim to name."

As they chatter with a steely zest,
Each knife knows it's simply the best.
But in the end, they all agree,
Their sharpness is what makes them family.

#beardboss

Memoirs of a Motorcycle Diary…

Thumping heart of steel, in rusted glory ride,
Up the rugged path where dreams and doubts collide.
Against the odds, you climb, relentless in your quest,
Old engine roaring loud, never seeking rest.

Each turn a victory, each breath a sigh,
As you conquer heights where the eagles fly.
With every beat, you tell a tale untold,
An old motorcycle, but a spirit bold.

To the top of the world, you make your stand,
Proof that even age can meet demand.
Through dust and storm, with courage unfurled,
You thump your way to the edge of the world.

#beardboss

House of Stars

Perched atop a hill so high,
A quaint house whispers to the sky,
Amidst the rain, in gentle light,
Golden lamps shimmer through the night.

Their glow, a dance on wet stone paths,
Flickers softly as the storm laughs,
Yet inside, warmth and quiet reign,
A peaceful refuge from the rain.

The world outside is lost in haze,
But here, the night becomes a maze,
Of light and shadow, soft and still,
A dream that crowns the quiet hill.

#beardboss

City Lights

In the heart of the night, a billion lights gleam,
Cities awake, lost in their neon dream.
Skyscrapers rise, their glimmers so bright,
Competing with the moon, in a silent fight.

But the full moon glows with a timeless grace,
Unmoved by the city's luminous race.
For in her soft, ethereal light,
She knows no match in the urban night.

Yet together they dance, in the velvet sky,
City lights and moonbeams, side by side.
A cosmic ballet, where both can shine,
In the endless tapestry of space and time.

#beardboss

Fleeting Amber's

Whispers of amber drift in the night,
From the heart of a bonfire, warm and bright,
They dance with the wind, a gentle flight,
Weaving tales of warmth in the cold moonlight.

Each spark a story, each glow a dream,
In the crisp winter air, they softly gleam,
Murmuring secrets, as they rise and beam,
A fleeting moment, like a silent stream.

Amber's glow fades, but the stories remain,
Lingering in the air, like a soft refrain,
On a winter night, by the fire's warm domain,
Where embers speak, and the heart feels no pain.

#beardboss

The Big Red Door

Beneath the full moon's silver gleam,
A door stands tall, caught in a dream,
Candles flicker, shadows play,
Guardians of night, they softly sway.

Wooden frame with carvings deep,
Secrets within, they quietly keep,
Mystical whispers, the wind's soft lore,
Echoes of realms beyond this door.

Step closer now, let your heart align,
For this is a portal where worlds entwine,
By moonlit glow and candle's dance,
Enter the mystery, take a chance.

#beardboss

Queen's Gambit

A silent face etched on the wall,
Amidst the chessboard's solemn call,
Black and white, the queen stands tall,
Yet in her reign, the shadows fall.

No words are spoken, none to tell,
In quiet corners, secrets dwell,
The queen moves with a steady grace,
But none can read the silent face.

Through battles won and games well-played,
The face remains, in shadows laid,
A timeless witness to each move,
As black and white in silence prove.

#beardboss

Rose Wall

Creepers of pink roses climb with grace,
Up the wall, they trace and chase,
Craving to peek through the window's frame,
To glimpse the world, to taste its flame.

They stretch and yearn, in silent plea,
For a view of skies, for what could be,
Their petals brush the glass so near,
Whispering dreams they long to hear.

But the window stays closed, still and cold,
While roses wait, their story untold,
Yet in their climb, they find delight,
In the hope of a view, in the soft dawn's light.

#beardboss

Ripples of Rain Drops

Ripples of raindrops dance and play,
On a blue pool where reflections sway,
Circles spreading in graceful arcs
As sky and water share their sparks

A gentle whisper in each wave
Echoes of the drops they gave
In liquid silver, blue meets grey
Where dreams in water softly lay

#beardboss

Moonlit Moon Shine Bar

Beneath the full moon's gentle gleam,
The Moonshine Bar begins to dream,
Its signage bathed in silver light,
A beacon in the velvet night.

Inside, where shadows softly play,
Stories weave, and laughter sways,
The music hums, a whispered tune,
As banter dances with the moon.

The night reveals what day conceals,
In moonlit corners, truth unseals,
With every note and every cheer,
The magic of the night draws near.

#beardboss

Tree by The Shore

On the seashore, a lone tree stands tall,
Gazing over rocks where waves gently fall,
As the golden hour paints the ocean's crest,
Earth and water unite, nature at its best.

Rocks bathe in the rhythm of the sea's embrace,
While the sun's glow crowns the ocean's face,
A symphony of life where elements meet,
In the harmony of earth and water, complete.

#beardboss

Red & Divine

In the quiet of a room, where shadows thin,
A bathtub spoke, its voice laced with a grin,
"Rose petals, oh, how delicate you lay,
In this gin-soaked bath, where we both sway."

The gin replied with a gentle clink,
"I dance with roses, as we sink and sink,
In this porcelain sea, where worlds collide,
A fragrant voyage where we both reside."

The roses sighed, "We float, we spin,
Entwined with the spirit of juniper and sin,
Our colors bloom, in the liquid's embrace,
Together, we find our secret place."

The bathtub chuckled, "What a pair we make,
A toast to moments we create and take,
For in this dance of rose and gin,
We weave a tale where indulgence begins."

#beardboss

Sun Kissed Frangipani

Beneath the blue, where white clouds drift,
A frangipani tree begins to lift,
Its blossoms bright, a golden hue,
Soaking up the sun, a sky so true.

Each petal unfolds, kissed by light,
In a dance with the day, soft and bright.
Rooted deep, yet reaching high,
It blooms in grace under the endless sky.

In this moment, pure and serene,
The frangipani stands, a tranquil queen,
Embracing warmth, with branches wide,
Beneath the sun, where dreams reside.

#beardboss

Boho by The Sea

In the golden hour's tender glow,
A bohemian girl, free and slow,
With sea wind weaving through her hair,
Dances with the twilight's care.

Her spirit wild, untamed and true,
As waves kiss sands in shades of blue,
She soaks the sun, a fleeting grace,
A wanderer in time and space.

The horizon whispers secrets near,
In her eyes, the world is clear,
A soul that drifts where dreams are spun,
She is the sea, the wind, the sun.

#beardboss

Waving Flag

On a sunlit shore where sand meets sea,
A flag flutters high, so wild and free,
Waving to waves with a gentle grace,
And nodding to clouds in their skyward chase.

It dances in rhythm with the ocean's breath,
Whispers of freedom in each fluttering crest,
As the sun bathes the day in a golden hue,
The flag sings its song to the vast and blue.

A silent salute to the winds that play,
A banner of hope in the light of day,
On this beach where land and sky entwine,
The flag flutters on, a timeless sign.

#beardboss

OTT - Old Town Tales

A vintage white Mercedes, timeless and grand,
Stands by the old town saloon, where memories
expand.
Its chrome glints in the sunlight, a regal display,
Whispers of past glories in its elegant array.

Once it roared through the streets, now it quietly
gleams,
A sentinel of history, guarding old dreams.
Parked in its prime, with stories untold,
A treasure in white, still shining like gold.

#beardboss

Reflections of A Heart

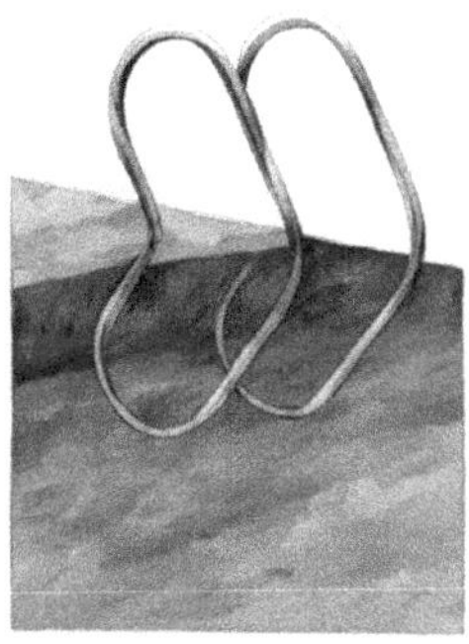

In a still pool, the heart's reflection lies,
A mirror of dreams beneath open skies.
Love whispers softly in the ripples' dance,
A timeless waltz, a sacred chance.

Every glance, every sigh, every tender stare,
Love blooms in the quiet, it's everywhere.
In the depths of the water, in the depths of the
soul,
Love's gentle touch makes the heart whole.

#beardboss

Stone Flower and Leaf

On a concrete block, a story unfolds,
A leaf and frangipani, in time's firm hold.
Immortalized in stone, their dance serene,
For centuries, they've kept their evergreen.

Petals and veins, etched deep, yet light,
A symbol of freshness, enduring the night.
In nature's embrace, they forever bloom,
Concrete cannot bind their eternal perfume.

#beardboss

Whirlpool of Time

Stepping into the whirlpool of time,
Where life's elements blend in a rhythmic chime,
Time and space dance, a fine-tuned spree,
In a swirl of fantasy, wild and free.

Moments converge, past and present entwine,
In this ride to remember, where dreams align,
A symphony of echoes, future and past,
Creating a melody that forever will last.

In the whirlpool's embrace, we find our place,
Where reality fades, and fantasies trace,
A path through the stars, a journey sublime.

#beardboss

Coconuts' Beachside Banter

By the beach, two coconuts swayed,
Watching humans in the sky parade.
"Look at them," one coconut said with a frown,
"Chasing clouds, yet bound to the ground."

The other chuckled, "They're a curious lot,
Wanting what they have not got.
In the sky, they yearn to be free,
But on the ground, they plant their dreams like trees."

"They want the stars, yet love the sand,
Building castles with trembling hands.
Up they soar, just to descend,
Seeking both the skies and earth's blend."

The coconuts sighed, swayed by the breeze,
"Humans," they mused, "are never at ease.
In the sky or on the land, they roam,
Forever searching for a place called home."

#beardboss

The Mystery Door

Behind this ancient door of stone,
Whispers of time in silence grown.
In shadows deep, the secrets lie,
Of laughter, tears, and a long-lost sky.

"The wood is worn, the hinges creak,
But echoes of the past still speak.
A world within, unseen, untold,
Guarded by the door so old."

"If you listen, lean in near,
The tales of yore you just might hear.
Of love and loss, of joy and pain,
Locked away, like whispers in the rain."

#beardboss

Skyfall

Sky Tower:
Oh, skies above, come closer still,
Let me kiss your endless will.
For in your arms, I long to stay,
In white and blue, we'll find our way.
I stand tall in white and blue,
Yearning to reach the skies, so true.
With every breeze that whispers by,
I stretch my hands, I dare, I try.
Blue Skies:
I see your wish, I feel your pull,
Your colors blend with mine so full.
But as you rise, so do I,
Forever distant, yet close, we lie.

White Clouds:
Between us both, I softly dance,
A fleeting touch, a mere romance.
I lace the skies, I crown your peak,
In this embrace, our love we seek.

#beardboss

Wings of Fire

In twilight's hush, where dreams ignite,
Wings of fire yearn for flight,
With embers bright and passion's blaze,
They stir the night, a fiery craze.

Bound to earth by tethered chain,
They shimmer with an untamed flame,
Their yearning whispers through the breeze,
To touch the skies, to find their ease.

The heavens call with a siren's plea,
"Unfold your wings, and follow me."
They brace for flight, for dawn's embrace,
To paint the sky with fiery grace.

So wait they do, in dreams' expanse,
For freedom's spark, for fate's advance,
Wings of fire, in shadows caught,
Ready to soar, to realms unbought.

#beardboss

Golden Hour

As the sun dips low and skies are gold,
I soar through clouds, their stories unfold.
Bathed in hues of twilight's grace,
The golden hour paints my space.

Whispers of the breeze in a celestial dance,
Golden threads weave dreams by chance.
Above the world where shadows lie,
I float through colors in the evening sky.

The sun's last kiss on wings of white,
Turns fleeting moments into light.
In this tranquil flight, the heavens' bloom,
I drift through dusk, in a golden room.

#beardboss

High on Chai

On peaks where clouds embrace the sky,
Where eagles soar and winds pass by,
In alpine hush where silence sings,
We share a cup, where sunlight clings.

The tea, a warmth against the chill,
Brews tales of heights and tranquil still,
With every sip, the world below,
Seems distant as the breezes blow.

High tea upon this lofty crest,
Where simple joys feel like the best,
A moment's peace, a fragrant climb,
In nature's grandeur, lost in time.

#beardboss

Talk of the Waves

Speed Boat:
"I cut through the waves, swift and sleek,
Leaving trails of white foam, bold and unique.
With engines roaring, I chase the horizon,
Racing past the caves where the past is frozen."
Long Tail Boat:
"I glide with grace, in rhythm with the sea,
My wooden frame echoes the island's decree.
I carry tales of yore, whispered by the wind,
Of Viking caves where secrets rescind."
Speed Boat:
"Your pace is gentle, but I thrive on speed,
In a rush for power, I fulfill the need.
But there's a charm in your steady stride,

A dance with the waves, a journey with pride."
Long Tail Boat:
"In your haste, you may miss the song,
Of the ancient cliffs where I belong.
For there's beauty in the slow, the unseen,
In the dance of shadows where I've always
been."
Speed Boat:
"Perhaps in my race, I forget the grace,
Of the timeless tides and the ocean's embrace.
As we surf this sea, we both belong,
In the echoes of the caves, our souls prolong."
#beardboss

Gleaming Corner

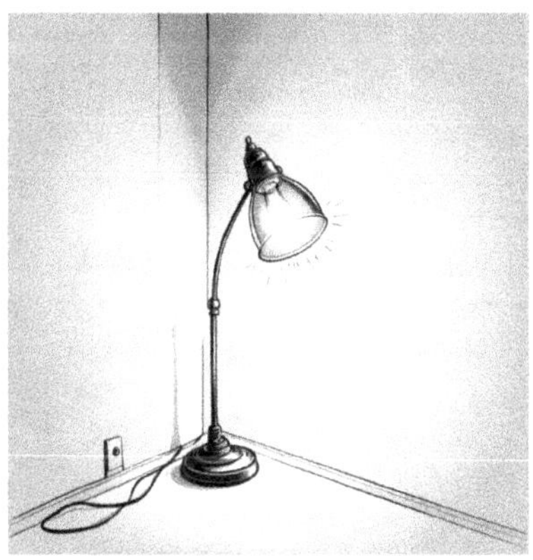

In a corner bright, where dreams ascend,
Adorned with lamps that softly blend,
Hot air balloons in vibrant hues,
Illuminate the night with mystic views.

Arabic script in golden glow,
Sheds light where warmest shadows flow,
A dance of colors, soft and grand,
As lanterns weave their magic strand.

In this nook where light takes flight,
Every lamp ignites the night,
A vibrant tale of dusk and dawn,
Where dreams and light forever fawn.

#beardboss

Golden Wings

As the sun dips low and skies are gold,
I soar through clouds, their stories unfold.
Bathed in hues of twilight's grace,
The golden hour paints my space.

Whispers of the breeze in a celestial dance,
Golden threads weave dreams by chance.
Above the world where shadows lie,
I float through colors in the evening sky.

The sun's last kiss on wings of white,
Turns fleeting moments into light.
In this tranquil flight, the heavens' bloom,
I drift through dusk, in a golden room.

#beardboss

Balance of The Stones

In stillness, stones find harmony,
Each balance a quiet decree.
Life, like rocks in careful pose,
Stands firm through highs and lows.

With patience, each stone aligns,
Echoing life's silent signs.
Steady hands and hearts entwine,
Crafting balance, pure and fine.

Each stone a story, weathered and true,
Teaching lessons in the view.
In balance, we find our way,
Stone by stone, day by day.

#beardboss

Knock to get Knocked over

In the hush of twilight's gentle breath,
A door stands hidden, veiled in depth.
Unlock it with your trembling hand,
To secrets, life has carefully planned.
Beyond the frame, where shadows dance,
A spark ignites, a bold romance.
Find your fire in the whispering night,
Where dreams and passions take their flight.
Let the flames reveal your hidden core,
Embrace the truth you've longed for.
In the heart of darkness, light will soar,
Opening the door to life's true lore.
For windows, once mere portals wide,
Now frame the world with hearts inside.
A simple pane, a clear divide,
Yet through it, worlds and souls collide.
Beyond the glass, life's tides may ride,
Yet here, we glimpse where dreams reside.

No longer just a view outside,
But love and warmth the light provides.
Through windows, now, connections glide,
A bridge where distant hearts confide.
In frames of wood and glass applied,
A universe where love abides.

#beardboss

Riding Waves of Life

On the crest of dawn, where the waves unfold,
Life's a surf on curves both young and old.
Concave dips where shadows steep,
And convex peaks where dreams leap.

Through hollowed hollows of the deep,
We carve our path, no chance to sleep.
Embracing both the highs and lows,
We ride the flow where the current goes.

In each thrilling turn and thrilling twist,
The ride is a dance of chance and risk.
So surf the swell with heart untamed,
Through concave dips and peaks unnamed.

#beardboss

Beach Please

On Patong's shore, I stand so still,
Draped in a dress, a beachy thrill,
Yet deep within, a silent plea,
To feel the sand beneath, set free.

Oh, how I long for waves' embrace,
The salty breeze to kiss my face,
But here I stay, a lifeless form,
Dreaming of warmth in a world so warm.

If only once, to dance, to sway,
With the tides that call, then fade away,
But I remain, in silence dressed,
A mannequin's dream, forever repressed.

#beardboss

Loop of Arches

In a world of arches, endless and bright,
We wander through day and into the night.
Each curve, a doorway, a passage so neat,
Leading us forward with every heartbeat.

From coffee shop arches to park gates so grand,
We walk through these portals, hand in hand.
Endless loops weave through mundane and
charm,
In arches, we find a magical calm.

They frame our journeys with secrets and grace,
In each arch, a story, a new embrace.
So here's to the arches that guide us each day,
In their endless loop, we find our own way.

#beardboss

Frangi-Pani

A frangipani perched high above,
Gazing down with silent love,
Days passed in wistful dream,
Of waters cool, a sparkling gleam.

At last, a gentle breeze took flight,
Carried the bloom through golden light,
It kissed the pool, a soft embrace,
A dance of ripples, a moment of grace.

Now it floats, a petal's sigh,
In the pool beneath the sky,
From longing gaze to liquid bliss,
A dream fulfilled in water's kiss.

#beardboss

Pillars of Time

In the deep world of cisterns, where shadows
dwell,
Ancient pillars whisper tales of time's spell.
Through water's veil and stone's embrace,
Forked lores of ages leave their trace.

Echoes of secrets, deep and profound,
In the stillness, where mysteries are found.
Each column bears the weight of years,
Holding time's stories, hopes, and fears.
In this hidden realm where darkness lies,
Pillars stand tall beneath silent skies.
Their stories intertwine, entwined and tight,
In the deep world of cisterns, lost at night.

#beardboss

Spooning up Life, Forking up the Fun

In the pages of life's grand tome, we find our way,
Forking up fun in the bright, joyous fray.
Spoonfuls of laughter, sweet moments to share,
Spoon in hand, we savor what's tender and rare.

Knifing out challenges with a resolute blade,
Cutting through shadows where doubts have stayed.
With each stroke, we carve paths anew,
Turning trials to triumphs, as dreams come true.

In this journal of life, with each written line,
We blend joy and struggle, like a well-crafted
wine.
Fork, spoon, and knife, our tools in this dance,
Creating a tale of life's grand romance.

#beardboss

Arc Reactor

In the heart's core, a spark ignites,
An arc reactor, glowing bright,
Within our souls, its light does grow,
A brilliance from which all radiance flows.

It's not the stars that light our night,
Nor distant suns with endless might,
But the ember deep within our chest,
A beacon of our inner quest.

From shadows cast, it breaks the chains,
Transforms our doubts and unseen pains,
In every breath and thought we find,
The power to illuminate the mind.

So let this glow, from deep inside,
Be the force with which we guide,
For it's within, our light does shine,
An arc reactor, pure, divine.

#beardboss

A Pensive Thought

In a frame of time, a statue stands still,
A pensive man lost in thoughts deep and still.
Eyes gazing outward, yet inward he roams,
In silence, he waits for souls to find home.

His stone visage, serene, holds a world unseen,
A realm of reflection where shadows convene.
Waiting, he stands as if time has paused,
For kindred spirits, in stillness, to cause.

Each moment he yearns for a presence to share,
To join in his reverie, a silent affair.
In the quiet expanse, where thoughts intertwine,
He waits in his frame for hearts to align.

#beardboss

Dancing with Sea Breeze

In a tranquil dance, where worlds entwine,
The sparkling ocean meets the golden tea's
shine.
Gentle waves hum secrets to the sunlit shore,
While the swaying tree whispers tales of yore.

Golden steam rises, a tender embrace,
As the ocean's sparkle mirrors the sky's grace.
In harmony's cradle, where time softly flows,
Tea, tree, and ocean in serene repose.

A tranquil symphony of nature's delight,
Where golden warmth and azure invite,
The soul drifts in this calming spree,
Where harmony reigns 'twixt tea, tree, and sea.

#beardboss

Brass Beauties

In a gleaming kitchen's warm embrace,
Brass pots and bowls, with a shining face,
Giggled and gleamed in joyous delight,
After a buffing that sparkled so bright.

"Look at us now, so polished and new!"
The pots chimed in, their voices in tune,
"We're gleaming like stars in the evening sky,
Shining so bright, we can't help but sigh."

The bowls, with a twinkle, softly replied,
"Your shine is so grand, it fills us with pride,
Together we sparkle, in the golden parade,
Our brilliance, a testament to the care we've
made."

Laughter rang out, a melodious cheer,
Their voices of joy for all to hear,
In the warmth of their shine, they danced and spun,
Brass pots and bowls, their gleaming hearts won.
#beardboss

Meow-nalisa

In the hush of an ageless gallery's gleam,
Where shadows dance in a timeless dream,
There sits a cat, with eyes so wise,
A Mona Lisa with feline guise.

Her gaze, a mystery veiled in grace,
A silent purr, a soft embrace,
Eternally poised in her quiet charm,
A portrait calm, devoid of harm.

Her whiskers whisper tales untold,
Of ancient nights and secrets bold,
In each serene and knowing stare,
She holds the world in quiet care.

Unchanging through the ages' flow,
Her enigmatic smile bestows
A tranquil peace, a timeless song,
In the heart of art where she belongs.

#beardboss

A Liquid Hug

On a rainy evening, soft and grey,
A cup of tea warms the chill away,
Its steam rises, a gentle mist,
A liquid hug that can't be missed.

Each sip a comfort, pure and bright,
A balm for the mind, a cozy light,
In the storm's embrace, we find our peace,
Tea's tender touch, a sweet release.

A companion true in nature's song,
With tea, the weary heart grows strong,
On cost rainy eves, it's love so plain,
A liquid hug for the waiting brain.

#beardboss

Pickle-a-Boo

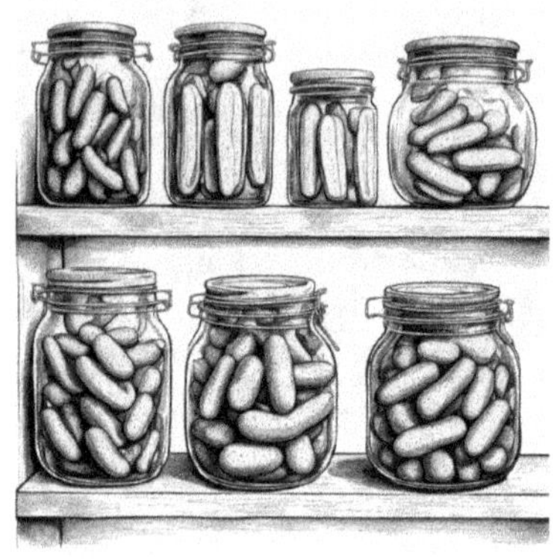

In a jar, a summer's sun preserved,
Yellow zucchini, in brine submerged,
On this rainy eve, I pause and see,
A golden warmth, in glass set free.

Rain taps softly on the windowpane,
Nature's rhythm, a gentle refrain,
Yet within this jar, a different light,
Glows through the gloom, a beacon bright.

Memories of gardens, of sunlit days,
Captured in the pickles' haze,
Crunch of harvest, now soft and sweet,
Transformed by time, a nostalgic treat.

The rain outside, a soothing song,
The jar, a summer that lingers long,
In each tender bite, a taste of cheer,
A whisper of warmth, when skies aren't clear.

#beardboss

Dark Brown Bromance

In a cozy corner of a coffee shop's embrace,
A fork, a cake, and a napkin convene with grace.
The fork, with gleaming prongs, speaks first
with delight,
"To slice this cake's sweet layers is pure joy
tonight."

The chocolate cake, rich with stories untold,
Replies with a crumbly voice, warm and bold,
"Each bite holds a secret, a decadent dream,
In every morsel, a rich, creamy gleam."

The napkin, soft and white, joins in the chat,
"With each crumb you collect, I'll make sure to
catch,
Your sweetness may linger, a moment to share,
On this ceramic plate, it's a sweet, simple
affair."

In their delicate dance, they weave a tale,
Of moments cherished, as time grows pale.
In the soft hum of the shop, where stories
collide,
A fork, a cake, and a napkin, in friendship,
abide.

#beardboss

Medusa's world

Beneath Istanbul's ancient, shadowed land,
Where time's soft whispers blend with stone,
In a cistern's cool and sunless hold,
Medusa's gaze is overthrown.

Her head, once fierce, now turned in sleep,
A silent sentinel of yore,
In murky depths where echoes creep,
She dreams of myths and tales of war.

For centuries in darkness deep,
Her serpents still in cold repose,
A timeless secret she does keep,
Where only moonlit waters flow.

Her power stilled, her rage untold,
Yet legends stir where waters run,
In Istanbul's embrace of old,
Medusa's head awaits the sun.

#beardboss

Fairy's Rope to Heaven

Beneath the evening's gentle sweep,
Where twilight dreams and shadows creep,
Lines of ropes and fairy lights,
Twine through the night, igniting sights.

Softly strung in stars' embrace,
Glimmers dance in cosmic grace,
Threads of warmth in the cool night air,
Whispers of enchantment rare.

Each flicker paints a fleeting glow,
On memories and moments flow,
In the tangled ropes of dreams so bright,
We find our way through the endless night.

#beardboss

Reflections of the High Pass

A mountain road, it winds so near,
Yet in the distance, it's unclear.
Reflections dance in morning's light,
A journey's end just out of sight.

Closer than it seems to be,
Yet far away, like memory.
The pass is closed, the path unknown,
But in the heart, it's fully grown.

A mirrored dream, a whispered call,
A step away, and still so small.
For every twist the mountain hides,
The road remains where hope abides.

#beardboss

www.ingramcontent.com/pod-product-compliance
Lightning Source LLC
LaVergne TN
LVHW020343200726
843507LV00012B/2481